Malik Ambar

From Slave to Sultan

Learn Hindi Through Stories

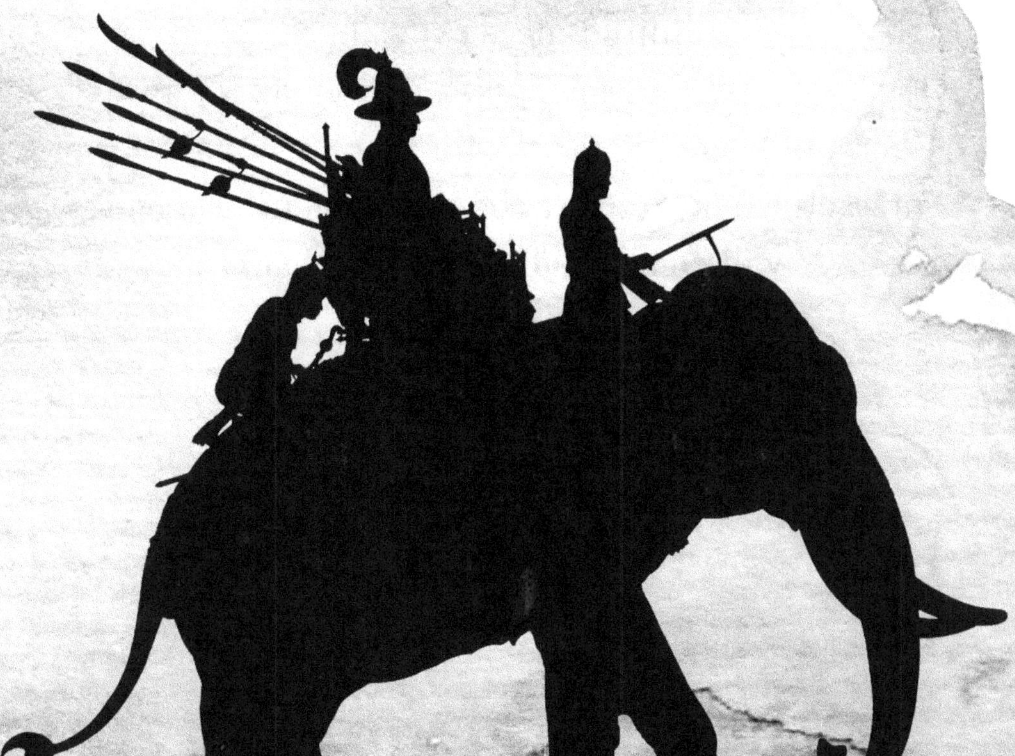

Thinkologie

Nicole Herbert Dean

What are Thinkologie Books?

We believe in teaching language via stories. Stories bring cultural context and display regional differences as well.
Each story will be in English as well as the target foreign language. Each storybook will have an interactive book to test comprehension. The books will be in Kindle and Paperback.

सिद्धी एक ५०,००० के करीब छोटा सा आदिवासी समुदाय है जो कर्नाटक और गुजरात के राज्यों और उनके आस पास के इलाकों में रहते हैं। यह समुदाय भारत में पाँचवीं या छठी शताब्दी में गुलामों के रूप में आया था। पुर्तुगाली और अरबी व्यापारियों ने इन्हें इथियोपिया, सोमालिया और पूर्व अफ्रिका के बंटू जनजातियों से चुना था।

इनकी शारीरिक ताकत और कौशल के वजह से इन्हें न चाहते हुए भी आना पड़ा। ये गुलामों को ले जाने वाले जहाज़ों पर सुरक्षा रक्षकों का काम करते थे और भयंकर समुद्री लुटेरों को जहाज़ पर कब्ज़ा करने से डराते थे। भारत के रियासतों के दरबारों में ये कुशल लोग अंगरक्षक, प्रशासक और सेना जैसी सेवाओं में भी कार्यरत थे।

मूल

ऐसे ही एक सिद्धि थे मलिक अंबर। मलिक का जन्म इथियोपिया के खंबाटा क्षेत्र में सन १५४८ में हुआ। ओरोमो नामक एक जातीय समूह का वे हिस्सा थे। भारत आने से पहले उनका उपनाम चापू था। इतिहासकार मानते है कि उनके माता पिता ने उन्हें गुलामी करने के लिए बेच दिया या फिर वे किसी युद्ध के दौरान पकड़े गए। इतिहासकार यह भी मानते है कि भारत आने से पहले सौदागरों और व्यापारियों ने इन्हें कई बार खरीदा और बेचा।

शिक्षा

इतिहासकार रिचर्ड एम. ईटन ने उनकी किताब अ सोशल हिस्टरी ऑफ़ द डेक्कन, १३०० - १७६१: एट इंडियन लाइव्स में बताया है कि उन्हें बगदाद के एक प्रमुख सौदागर को बेचा गया था, जिसने उनकी बौद्धिक क्षमता और शारीरिक कौशल को पहचाना। इस सौदागर ने उन्हें पढ़ाया और उन्हें इस्लाम धर्म में परिवर्तित किया और उन्हें अंबर नाम दिया।

१५७० के शुरुआत में चंगेज़ खान नामक शासक, जो कभी खुद गुलाम थे, मलिक अंबर को खरीदा और उन्हें अहमदनगर सल्तनत के दक्कनी पठार में ले गए.

सत्ता में उठना

मलिक को खरीदने के पाँच साल बाद चंगेज़ खान गुज़र गए।

दक्कन के गुलामी के नियमों के अनुसार अब मलिक आज़ाद थे।

इतिहासकार मनु पिल्लै लिखते है कि इसी दौरान मुग़ल सम्राट अकबर की दृष्टि दक्कनी पठार पर पड़ी। यहीं से मलिक अंबर सत्ता में बढ़ते गए। उन्होंने पड़ोसी रियासत से हाथ मिलाया और ३००० योद्धाओं की फ़ौज जुटा ली जो सन १६०० में ७००० योद्धाओं तक बढ़ी, जिनमें दक्कनी और मराठा भी शामिल थे। यह फ़ौज बहु-नस्लीय और बहु-जातीय थी।

ज़रूरत के अनुसार ताकत और युक्ति का चतुराई से प्रयोग करके अहमदनगर राज्य में अंबर एक प्रमुख ताकत के रूप में उभरे। पिल्लै लिखते है कि जब वे अपनी ताकत के शिखर पर थे तब पश्चिमी दक्कन के निज़ाम शाही को साफ़-साफ़ अंबर की जागीर कहा जाता था।

विरासत की स्थापना

अहमदनगर में मुगलों को हराकर और उनको पीछे हटने को मजबूर करने के बाद, मलिक ने खिरकी नामक राजधानी स्थापित की। आज उसे औरंगाबाद के नाम से जाना जाता है। उन्होंने जल घर, भूमिगत नहरें और घर बनाए। औरंगाबाद में उन्होंने जामा मस्जिद और काली मस्जिद भी बनाए और मालगुज़ारी वसूल करने के लिए एक व्यवस्था बनाई।

मलिक की मृत्यु सन १६२६ में हुई। उनकी कब्र खुल्दाबाद में है। महान मराठा योद्धा शिवाजी ने उनके महाकाव्य शिवभारत में मलिक की जीवन गाथा का गौरव करते हुए उन्हें सूरज की तरह बहादुर बताकर संबोधित किया।

सम्राट जहाँगीर के दिन पत्रिका लिखने वाले, मुतम्मिद खान, जो मलिक के प्रखर प्रतिद्वंद्वी थे, वे मलिक के बारे में लिखते हैं कि युद्ध में, आदेश देने में, सही फैसला लेने में और प्रशासन करने में कोई भी उनकी बराबरी नहीं कर सकता था। एक अबीसीनिया के गुलाम का इतनी ऊँचाई पर उठने का कोई और दूसरा वाकयात इतिहास में दर्ज नहीं है।

The Story of Malik Ambar
From Slave to Sultan

Malik Ambar is a notable character who is part of

India's history. Not much is known about him, but he is

a person worth writing about. He faced struggles but

overcame them. His story is unusual and encouraging!

Origins

The Siddis are a small **tribal community** of approximately 50,000 people residing in the states of Karnataka, Gujarat and **surrounding** areas. These tribes came to India in the 5th/6th century as **slaves**. Portuguese and Arab **traders** picked them from the Bantu tribes of Ethiopia, Somalia, and East Africa.

They involuntarily came because of their **physical strength** and **skills** . They worked as **security** guards aboard the slave ships, intimidating the **fiercest pirates** from taking over. These skilled men also served as **bodyguards**, **administrators**, and **military** in the courts of the **princely** rulers of India.

One such Siddi was Malik Ambar. Malik was born in Ethiopia in the Khambata region in 1548. He was part of an **ethnic group** known as the Oromo. His nickname was 'Chapu' before he came to India. **Historians** believe his parents sold him into slavery or that he was **captured** during a war. They also believe **merchants** and traders bought and **sold** him **several times** before he arrived in India.

Education

According to the historian, Richard M Eaton, in his book 'A Social History of the Deccan, 1300–1761 Eight Indian Lives', he was sold in Baghdad to a **prominent** merchant who recognized his **intellectual** abilities and his **physical prowess.** This merchant **educated** him and **converted** him to Islam, and gave him the name, 'Ambar'.

In the early 1570's a **former** slave turned

ruler, Chengiz Khan, bought Malik Ambar and

took him to the sultanate of Ahmednagar, in

the Deccan Plateau. Chengiz Khan died five

years after he **purchased** Malik. At this time

Malik was free, **according to** the **rules** of

slavery in the Deccan.

Rise to Power

The historian Manu Pillai wrote that the Mughal emperor Akbar had his **sights** on the Deccan **plateau** at this precise time. This was when Malik Ambar rose to power. He joined forces with a **neighboring** lord and gathered a force of 3000 **warriors**, which grew by the 1600s to 7000 warriors including Dakhnis and Marathas. This army was **multi-racial** and **multi-ethnic**.

What other's say

"**Cleverly**, using **muscle** when it was needed and **trickery** when that suited his ends, Ambar emerged as the **principal force** in what used to be the Ahmednagar state. At the height of his power, it was said that the Nizam Shahi of the western Deccan was simply referred to as 'Ambar's land." Pillai writes.

Establishing Legacy

After **defeating** and **forcing** the Mughals to retreat from Ahmednagar, Malik **established** a capital called Khirki. It is known as Aurangabad today. He built waterworks, **underground canals,** and houses. He also built the Jama Masjid and the Kala Masjid in Aurangabad and established a model for **land revenue.**

Malik died in 1626. His **mausoleum** is in Khuldabad.

While celebrating his life, Shivaji, the great Maratha leader, referred to Malik as 'brave as the sun' in his epic poem, Sivabharata.

Mutamid Khan the diarist of Emperor Jahangir, a fierce opponent of Malik, wrote this about him, "He had no equal in **warfare**, in **command**, in **sound judgment**, and **administration**. History records no other instance of an Abyssinian slave arriving at such **eminence**."

INDIA
Deccan Plateau
Ahmednagar

Note: Please use Hindi words for all activities, even though we have provided a translation.
It is important to annotate the words you do not know by underlining and highlighting them.
There is a vocabulary bank at the end of the book to guide you.

Mark the Text

Use the following strategies to mark the text.

 Circle content and look up the words in dictionary.com

 Put a question mark near words that need explanation.

 When did this story take place?

 Where did this story take place?

 What is the theme of this story?
e.g. love, slavery, war

Sorting Activity

Read the text. Find and place the words in the box

Nouns	Proper Nouns
Abstract Nouns	Collective Nouns
Definite article	Indefinite article

Sorting Activity

Read the text. Find and place the words in the box

Adverbs	Verbs
Adjectives	**Prepositions**
Punctuation	**Superlatives**

Questions

Select the correct choice by circling the letter or fill the blanks

The Siddies are a ________________________________ community.

a. tribal
b. school
c. trader

The Siddies live in ________________________________.

a. Karnataka, Gujurat
b. Ethiopia, Somalia
c. in India

The Siddies came to India in the __________ century.

a. 5th or 6th
b. 7th and 8th
c. 4th and 5th

The ________________________________brought them
as slaves.

a. Portuguese and Arab traders
b. Ethiopian and Somalian traders
c. Siddi traders

Questions

**Select the correct choice by circling the letter or fill
the blanks**

The Siddies were chosen because of their_________ _______________.

a. physical strength and skills
b. physical strength
c. skills

The Siddies worked as ____

a. bodyguards,
b. military
c. all of the above

The Siddies worked in the __________ ____________________________.

a. courts of the rulers
b. slave ships
c. all of the above

The name of a famous Siddi was _________ ___________________.

a. Malik Ambar
b. Mr. Siddi
c. Jehangir

Questions

Select the correct choice by circling the letter or fill the blanks

Malik Ambar was educated by a ________ ________ from Baghdad.

a. wealthy merchant
b. prominent merchant
c. smart teacher

His master gave him the name __________________________ .

a. Oromo
b. Ambar
c. Chapu

The ruler _________ _____________brought him to the Deccan.

a. Ghengiz Khan
b. Chengiz Khan
c. Jehangir Khan

The name of the town was _________________.

a. Ahmedabad
b. Ahmednagar
c. Aurangabad

Questions

**Select the correct choice by circling the letter or fill
the blanks**

Malik Ambar rose to power ___________ __________ ___________________.

a. when his master died
b. by killing his master
c. learning how to fight

His army grew from ____

a. 3000 to 7000
b. 3000 to 6000
c. 3000 to 5000

His army was _______________ and_______________________.

a. Multi racial and multi ethnic
b. Dakhnis and Marathas
c. Mughals and Marathas

He defeated the _______________.

a. Marathas
b. Mughals
c. Dakhnis

Questions

Select the correct choice by circling the letter or fill the blanks

Malik Ambar _____________ and _________the Mughals to retreat.

a. defeated and forced
b. challenged and defeated
c. fought and defeated

He established a capital called _______________________________

a. Khirki
b. Ahmednagar
c. Aurangabad

He built the _______________ and_______________________.

a. Jama Masjid and Kala Masjid
b. Lal Kila and Taj Mahal
c. Jama Masjid and Taj Mahal

He built _______________ and _______________ _______________.

a. Waterworks and underground Canals
b. Many buildings
c. Waterworks and buildings

Create a One Pager

Draw and Label the Story

Vocabulary Bank

आदिवासी समुदाय	इतिहासकार
आस - पास का	पकड़े
गुलाम	व्यापारी
व्यापारी	बेचा
शारीरिक ताकत	बहुत बार
कौशल	प्रमुख
सुरक्षा	बौद्धिक
समुद्री लुटेरे	कौशल
अंगरक्षक	शिक्षित
प्रशासक	धर्मान्तरित
सैन्य	भूतपूर्व
राजसी	शासक
जातीय समूह	खरीदा

Vocabulary Bank

के अनुसार	हराने के बाद
नियम	जबरदस्ती
गुलामी	वापसी
दृष्टि	स्थापित
पठार	भूमिगत नहरें
पड़ोसी	भू राजस्व
योद्धा	समाधि
बहु-नस्लीय	युद्ध
बहु-जातिय	नियंत्रण
बड़ी चतुराई से	ध्वनि निर्धारण
मांसपेशी	प्रशासन
प्रवंचना	श्रेष्ठता
प्रमुख बल	

Contact us

Our mission is to help other educators, coaches and homeschoolers also!
Contact us for customized interactive books. If you want to publish your book - contact us for that too!
Follow our author page
https://amazon.com/author/thinkologiebooks
We are also on Instagram @thinkologie
Twitter @ thinkologie
Facebook @thinkologiemedia

Thinkologie